Rajani

Rajani

Or, Songs of the Night

Dhan Gopal Mukerji

MINT EDITIONS

Rajani: Or, Songs of the Night was first published in 1922.

This edition published by Mint Editions 2021.

ISBN 9781513299976 | E-ISBN 9781513223438

Published by Mint Editions®

 MINT
EDITIONS

minteditionbooks.com

Publishing Director: Jennifer Newens
Design & Production: Rachel Lopez Metzger
Project Manager: Micaela Clark
Typesetting: Westchester Publishing Services

To A— C—
with friendship and gratitude

Contents

Foreword

In writing these poems, the spirit and the music of my own language, Bengali, have overlapped the English meter. No desire for experiment has created them. They came. . . in the shadow-light garment of the dying day. . . in the image of my own belovéd Bengal.

Dhan Gopal Mukerji

Introduction

I n this little volume a young Hindu scholar has tried to express in English "free verse" something of the dream-poetry of his native Bengal. The little poems are not translations, nor imitations. They are fancies of the night, "Rajani," suggestions and bints of the emotions which the darkness awakens in the mind of a mystical scholar. In the first of the series, "Bhikshu" (mendicant), the poet, feels himself awakening as a suppliant for reality in the light of Oriental thought. With the dawn, he bails the Lotus, "Om Moni Padme Om," as the symbol of the source whence flows the "nectar of sustenance," the life-impulse which vivifies all living creatures.

"Rajani," the world of baffling dreams, showers down its strange sensations, but with all these goes the bidden sense of lack of reality. Through the morning dew comes the song of the "Bhikshu," the lute-player who has lost his scroll and makes his plea for reality.

For the rest, the verses must tell their own story. It remains for me to say, that Dhan Gopal Mukerji was born near Calcutta in 1890, that he was educated in the Universities of Calcutta, Tokyo, California and Stanford, taking his degree at Palo Alto, in 1914, as a student of Comparative Literature.

David Starr Jordan

Stanford University,
February 18, 1916.

*Bhikshu's Song

A Bhikshu at the door,
Om Moni Padme Om!
A lute-player without a scroll;
A boatswain without his toll.
My barque is laden with life,
Bound for the shore of light;
Let it drift with the stream
To its destination of dream!

A Bhikshu at the door,
Om Moni Padme Om!
A singer that sings of sorrow;
Whose night knows no tomorrow;
My song finds its source
In its moonless immensity
Bound with the girdle of sleep;
Love's Nirvana, the only pearl in its deep.

Bhikshu, singer, sorrower,
I see the face of thy star;
Om Moni Padme Om!
A barque of life with love,
O, guide thou from above,
With thy star-music's silver tone,
Om Momi Padme Om!

---

* Buddhist monks are called Bhikshus.

Song of the Stars

Sailing unseen
On sapphire wing,
Linked together with unseen chain;
Silently swinging,
Noiselessly smiling,
Bear we the moon's far-sweeping train.
She like a queen
Of queenliest dreams,
Stepping upon the cloudy stair,
Mounts to her throne
To man unknown,
In the heaven's blue heart bare.
With slender hands,
The meteor bands
Sway the cloud-fans many;
Then we seek
The ocean's deep,
In its endless symphony,
For hidden treasures
In its chambers,
To adorn the moon's bright crown;
While the other stars
Search afar,
Over green lands and pools of brown.
The night's heart,
That covers the earth,
Embraces heaven, earth and sea;
Her fair daughters,
The moon and the stars,
Are her smile, mirth, and revery.
With love endless,
Her mother's breast
Pours incessant nectar white,
For us to drink;
For us to bring
To man, praying for the graces of night.

On her lap,
Silently nap
Green-tressed plant and trees;
In her arms
That dream embalms,
Rest so many children like bees.
And their souls
Their wings unfold,
Course with the moon and us,
From sunset's bank
To sun-dawn's strand
That twilight joins like an isthmus,
The two continents
Of time's moments
Known as night and day;
Light our smile,
Night our wile,
The sun's light and the moon's ray.
Through infinite space,
At phantom's pace,
Move we without end;
With opal laughter,
We make and mar
Destiny's good and evil bent.
With perfumed kiss
On youth's sweet lips,
Open we the checkered doors of dream;
With gem and coral,
We make the coronal
That from love's brow doth send its gleam
Through all darkness,
Like a largess
To descend, dance and scatter
Over mountain-crest,
The valley's breast,
Its glory in gold and silver.
Then life and love
We lift silently above
For blessing, from earth yonder,

To night's cathedral
That has many a portal
With votaries of dream and star.
First they enter
Their tribute render
At sleep's silent hall;
Then silently pace,
With humble grace,
Where the fairies install
Queen fancy,
Her necromancy,
On her throne in child's soul.
Then they pass
With awesome hush
To that portal where, whorl
Rising on whorl
Of smoke of gold,
Floating on saffron wing
Colors the arch
The columns march
And cloud-fans that meteors swing.
From behind the altar,
Like a million star,
Wakes the Sungod at last!
We dance and sing
The primal hymn
To the cloud-herald's trumpet blast.
Lo, the king rises!
Shadow vanishes,
Thrilling all with light and joy,
The glacial mountain,
And limpid fountain
That runs adown it like a boy,
With message of light
On lips snow-white
To the sleeping valley beneath.
Then to the ocean,
That with commotion
Its waking breath doth heave.

Our song is over,
We fly yonder,
With mother night and moon,
To distant lands,
In myriad bands,
Where all are restfully aswoon.

Rasha Measure

A Dance of the Autumn Festival of India

The champak* showers its perfume from the trees;
The lotus petals athrill with the breeze,
The pellucid pool a magic mirror for beauty,
And the faun-breeze pipes in Rasha measure, for Thee.
Dance, my Radha! Thy lac-dyed feet, tiny red birds
Free, though caged by thy will, like the bard's
Songs chained to the ivory throne of Poesy,
That with delight they bear, like thy feet, thy golden body—
Dance of love that is born not to live.
Trip, trip, O lotus feet!
Let them weave, weave a dream
That will outmatch the march of eternity.
Who wants eternity? When death's fantasy,
That dwells in thy smile, in the artistry
Of thy arms, thy snake-black hair,
That chides and laughs to the limpid air?

Daughter of mirth,
Merry mover of man's heart,
Songstress of heaven on earth,
For one moment, dance upon my heart.
Oh! It keeps time, though not knowing how—
With thine anklets ringing, now loud, now low,
Again so fast. Why so fast?
Are they breaking, as my heart?
Cease not dancing, though death is at my door!
Stop not laughing, though I hear no more!
Let thine eyes twinkle, shine without end;
God's face they mirror, that makes death wend

---

* Champak is a soft yellow aromatic flower.

His way afar, far away from thee
With the moon's setting as the tide of the sea.
Yet I die, die—to live: under the champak tree,
Where the breeze pipes in Rasha measure for thee.

TARA-BINDU

As the breeze falls asleep,
The brush of sunset
Draws the rosy cloud-scape
On the canvas of the sky;
The blue hills in repose
Listen to the pearl lullaby of the mist.

A song of dimming light, this,
And dance of shadows with silver feet,
For the joy of one shy star-maid
Seeking hiding from the moon
Behind the emerald screen of the sea.

Evening Star

Many a twilight hour,
Gazing at thee, I wonder
What might thine name be,
Thou resplendent star?
As the crimson sun
Sinks behind the cirque of rocks,
Like a spark of hope
To cheer the desolate hour,
Thou arisest, dream-maiden of night;
Thy rays, pulsating through
The throbbing heart of time,
Outreach the boundless shores of space.
My soul amazed, I gaze and gaze
To fathom thy depths. I dare not!
Yet through the latticed bars of life,
Thy soul I seek, transcendent flower of night!

Following the Light

Your smile hath called me mutely,
    Like the lingering light
That beckons the shy and silent star
    To follow her
Mate behind the sky, beyond the bar.

I listened to your urgent call
    Echoed by the empty vault
Where ascends my soul like the mute star,
    And like her
I follow your smile, but reach you never.

Ah, vain the search! fruitless my toil!
    My eyes are dimmed, see not
Far, nor near;
    Like the paling star,
I fall, I faint. . . "Come!" . . . Never!

Her Poet

Many a bard
   Sang many a song;
Many a dreamer
   Dreamt many a dream;
Many a smile
   Cast many a beam;
Many a lover
   Loved, eternal, long.

But no life
   Lived like his;
None sang
   Sweet like him;
None loved
   Love like him;
No love
   True as his.

To Beauty

Faithful I be or not to thy soul-call,
    Yet thou awaitest at my door,
In winter's spotless white, or summer's
    Gold-green-crimson garb;
Ever smiling thy lips, tearfully sweet thine eyes!
    Constancy—ah! how vain a word!
Too little like a star to contain all of night's majesty!
    What shall I name thy love, O goddess?
Deep in my dark heart I moan for nothing,
    Shed tears for what can not be,
Like the unwished-for rain of summer, that weeps uselessly.
    Cruelly I lie, I lie hidden,
While thou waitest for me through an eternity
    Of heart-breaking expectancy:
At last I come, mine eye hath seen thy glory,
    Thy rose-red, love-kindling lips,
Thine eyes, dark like the heart of night,
    Two homes of immortal mystery.
I come, contrite, weeping, forgiven;
    Let my lips kiss thy dove-like feet,
My heart's perfume pour I on them,
    And my soul set to song
Thy song, endless song, from earth to heaven
    Like a sky-rover's at dawn.

The night builds her temple of rain:
In the forest a sobbing music
Played by the hands of darkness
On the scale of dark leaves.

No bird-song stirs the soul;
Nor the golden dawn-harmonies;
A cry, a shedding of tears,
A music of sable tonalities.

Truly, a temple of silence and sound,
A vibrant, and dim solitude,
A gray telling of black beads;
A prayer, a moan, a dim worship.

The rain builds a bridge
    Between the sky and the sea;
The breeze sings his beggar-song
    From the brine to the lea;
A lone tree, solitary pilgrim,
    Waits on the shore of the deep
To walk on the steps of waves strewn with rain-flowers,
    Up to the temple of Eternal Sleep.

*The Tower of Silence

Silent! Tread airily!
    Hush, pilgrim!
Lay your tribute softly,
    They sleep, they sleep. . .
The dwellers of this tower lonely.

From life's path tortuous,
    Travelled they
To this solemn house that towers
    Its head
To the heavens' eternal bowers.

Pray soulfully, mutely,
    Kneel reverently,
Utter no word, sadly, coldly,
    Walk hence humbly.

They sleep, the dead,
    In that tower;
Laying their burdened heads
    At God's feet,
As they lie at rest on the couch of death.

Silent! Tread airily!
    Hush, pilgrim!
Lay your tribute softly—
    They sleep, they sleep. . .
The dwellers of this tower lonely.

Ah, have they spoken to thee
    A soundless word?
Weep not, though to live is to weep,
    Ah, gently, gently,
Walk hence reverently!

---

* The Zoroastrians, instead of burying their dead, leave them in the Tower of Silence.

Nisha

I fell asleep,
    Hearing melody
That fell from lip to lip.
    The stars sang it
To the wind, that took it
    To the rose, shivering in the cold of night.

The rose gave it
    To the nightingale, who sang it
Back to the stars, the earth and the sea.
    And I, to it listening;
Fell asleep dreaming.

NOTE:—From the author's own Bengali.

Before the Buddha at Kamakura

Dead, thou never art,
Though no breath stirs thine armored form,
Thy bronzed lips not a word do speak.
All these years, two thousand and more,
What hast thou seen—thine eyes closed?
What hast thou been feeling, senseless body!
All thy luminous dreams hid from mankind's ken?
Yet would I give thee all I am,
If, for a moment, these eyes could see
What thou seest eternally.

Why sad, like a crushed flower,
Thy smile-adorned face?
They, the sparkling rays
That the dawn of day
Sends through the silent trees,
Have they hurt thee?

Cease not to smile—
The sun will set soon,
The darkness fall,
"Ave Maria" sing the breeze.

Then, my soul's sovereign deity,
Through the long, long hours of night,
Made bright with the moon's light,
We will hold our tryst.

Take these flowers
God's beloved child,
Receive them kindly;
Though they are wild,
They grew in my heart
That bleeds for thee.
Why art thou making
A garden of roses?
Art thou forgetting?
Have I brought roses
From thine own garden,
Red with the bloom of love?
Sun-flower I bring;
It is the day of love's birth.
The garden is athrill
With song and mirth:
Oh, take all, fruit and flower
And that lotus—my soul!

LOVE'S CORONATION

Thou and I,
In the world of stars,
Where no limit the limitless mars:
Thou and I afar,
Beyond the smile of the star
Beyond the sun's many-colored bar.
In the bosom of night,
Beyond the lunar dart,
I will enthrone thee queen of my heart.

To the Sun Shore

(After Hearing a Bengali Song)

Fill with the breeze of hope
The unfurled sail of your boat!
O maiden, row, row on faster, row!
There dances the golden cloud,
Where the sea kisses the sky blue—
O maiden, row faster, row!

The witches laugh behind;
Yonder lies the haven of light;
Before the light of love doth cease,—
Look! The birds, like argonauts,
Sail in quest of the golden cloudy fleece;—
Before the sun closes his eyes,
Speechless swain of my bark, row, row
Beyond, beyond the gold-cloud's bar.

The fairies dance in the forest of Song;
Silver cymbals ring in the grove of dreams;
Round the islet of green fancies,
Beyond the world's barren promontory,
Bring your sunset barque,
With pilgrims from the land of Life.

The stars mingle their tears of joy
With the mellow effulgence of the moon;
The Song-birds wake, thinking it day,
And pour their hearts in accord with a luminous tune.

Oh, come to the Forest of Forgetting!
Play the lutes of your soul evermore!
Thrid on the harp of sorrow's heart;
Let joy-notes through the lyre-strings pour.

Dance, ye fairies from the valley of sleep!
Trip, O rose-feet, in moonlight dipped!
Let waves of the stream of notes
Wash the sky with golden tones;
For ye to minuet up the moon-set hills,
Where silent mist makes silver music.

The honey-colored moon,
Washed in silver;
The stars, luminous clusters of
Grapes, hung from invisible vines.

Ah, were I a daring mariner,
I would sail on the barge of the moon
To the far island of God's mirth,
Where they drink star-wine,
And dance to the music of the spheres.

A Drama

This deep yet unfilled night
    Has rites;
A worship, a dance, and speech;
A passion play of leaves and light,
    Singing and sounding
Without noise, without life,
Of its own immense intangibility,
"Trance-bedimmed" and silence-bright.

White mist wings the pink-draped sky;
Gold clouds kiss the blue mountain crest;
Song-birds soar and mock their love with laughter and cry!
The baby smiles in silver joy
To the stars' silent, flower-like call.
Mother whispers with tulip-lips, pearl-tears filling her eyes.
The Child
Sees not; dream has closed his ivory lids,
With the sun's sinking into the ocean of sleep.
*The crescent flings in a mood of mirth his drapery of purple and stars;
The gray arm of the mist embraces the valley and the dark.
The Song-bird has ceased; the tulip closed its lips.
All is still
Save the breeze,
Fanning the world to sleep.

---

* The moon is "masculine" in Bengali.

AFTER READING YONE NOGUCHI

Between the rose garden
    And the sunset,
    I sought my beloved.
Between the dawn's blush
    And night's star;
Between dream's arm and
    Sleep's embrace,
    I sought my belovéd,
Between the rose garden and the sunset.

Gold and rose the colors held in
    The palette of the sky,
For the sun-bar paint-brush
    Of nature to paint with these
His sunset, on His blue
    Heavens, and green-blue hills.

The mountain peaks, a halted army,
Helmeted with gold and green;
The sea before them a veil of pink
That the moon casts away,
To wear the gold-violet robe of mist
Before entering the Shrine of night.

Coral-music, the sunset writes on the scroll of the sea;
Gold strings are strung in the harp of the sky;
Cloud-fingers, playing on them,
Make noiseless gossamer-melody;
As the amber-draped moon-maid
Trips from the sea to the Heavens
Dancing the measure of evening worship.

Lunar Rainbow

The moon spreads a rainbow fan
With her beams, and the cloud
Puts on it one star. . .
A song within a dream.
What moon-maid after dance,
On what balcony standing,
Cools her face with this fan,
The star holding a mirror to her eyes?

The New Buddha

The moonbeams, like intangible flowers;
The air, the trembling drapery of the priest;
The murmur of the river, a soft chant. . .
All are there at the feet of Night,
The white Buddha on the shore of Sleep,
Brooding over a new Nirvanic peace.

The silence of enlightenment, a new ecstasy,
Calls our souls like bees
To suck honey from the lotus of Eternity.
A perfection this, of silence, of peace and light;
Night, the only Buddha that attains to it.

The sun waters the pastures of heaven
  With warm rains of light;
For the golden-lambkins to graze. . .
  The star-flocks of night.

Memory of Childhood Days

A pain become pleasure;
    A silence become song;
Sorrow moving to joy's measure;
    A night gold-draped as dawn.

The pink adornéd heavens;
    The low tone of the breeze;
A little child star-gazing—
    The mariner of dreams' deep seas.

Oh, the gladness that comes here,
    When memory brings the hour in
Through the portals of reverie,
    When the one star doth the sun bedim.

Indeed, a gladness born of sadness,
    Those days held in memory's sieve
Like numberless gems from Time's mine,
    That their mother-mine outlive.

Ah, sleep-ravished eyes
Dream of a paradise,
That close to our heart lies,
Sleep-ravished eyes.

Peace and pleasure,
Their music and measure;
Love and love's treasure,
Oh, peace in pleasure!

Eyes dark and deep;
All dreams they keep
In their labyrinths of sleep;
Oh, eyes dark, deep!

Forbid me not
To come to your side of the stream;
The water from yours
Naughtily flows into mine.
My pitcher refuses
To hear the gurgle of your water;
Yet, it mysteriously fills
Its every corner, till all soundless is;
Like your love
Wordless, filling the cup of my life.

It is but coming and going;
Laughing or weeping;
In dark or day!
Life is but a lay:
Rings sad or gay,
Depending on our singing.

The Heart of a Song

The sun glints the waves with silver;
The gull, a white butterfly of desire;
The barque, a fancy of some intoxicated singer.

The brown islets, lost souls from the world of song;
The wind, an ever-sounding, unseen gong,
Telling of the worship of the sun, the sea and the storm.

Blue, brown, silver, song, sound and storm;
Dreams of a dying hour, shadow of a morn
That we have seen mirrored in the heart of song.

Storm Worship

The cloud-cymbals make the music of the thunder;
The lightning-maid dances to its measure;
While the breeze-devotees sing their prayer.

A worship of lunatics, this;
God-mad souls seeking peace;
Dervishes, whose agony knows no surcease.

No many-color-robéd priest is here;
No conch-shell's flourish and blare;
No frankincense, myrrh, or perfume rare.

A worship of passion and powers;
A benediction of liquid flowers
Poured through a million silver showers.

To my heart's garden, stealthily
    Came he
To steal the rose that bloomed in it.
    Ah, thief!
I caught him, hand, head and heart;
Smile! Cry! a robber, thou art!
    Ah, me—
Who caught whom, He—me?

ERNEST DOWSON

By the limpid pool at twilight,
    Sat he
Wearily watching its slumberous deep,
    Like his sad soul,
    For jeweled fishes?
Like the phantoms of his dreams,
That elude imagination's reach;
Like those airy beings far-soaring overhead
    In the
Pale-colored, star-crowned height?
A faint smile lay on his pale lips,
    Like the
Last, low, lingering light
    That slides
Adown the inverted cup of blue,
    To make room for her,
    The shining star.
Gently drooped his golden head;
As the pool drew its veil of black,
    He fell asleep,
By the woodside green and dark.

Sedan Bearer's Song

Star of our dream,
    Flower of our song;
Carry her tenderly,
    Carry her on.

Light of our life,
    Soul of our love;
On the wings of air,
    Bear her above.

Undying light,
    Unsetting star,
Flower of immortality,
    Heart of our love.

With the breath of perfume,
    Warm and rare,
Bear her joyously,
    Bear her fair.

The soul of day migrates into the night;
The moon on the eastern hill;
The sound of work seeks repose
Through sunset's silence, into deeper silence still!
No dark this eve, but a silver flow
Washing from the sky the dusty sunset glow,
Then mount it with a soft star—
A reflection of God's eye in Heaven's mirror.

THE MADMAN

Was it a wayside flower,
Or was it her face,
Made thee mad, brother?
Or a madness grown apace
With a love that sought
The image of its soul
That with life cannot be bought;
Nor death's eternal roll
Of days and moving years
Can take it out of memory's bourne?

'Twas not love. . . maybe, hate
That made thy heart mad;
Hurled thee in this state!
O brother! be not sad;
Madness the guerdon of the gods
To those that sought gladness,
And forgot Fate that lords
Over Love's life and largess;
Give us, yes, what we seek. . .
Alas! not as we need, but as they see fit.

Sorrow not, though it pains thee.
Laugh! thou laughest as mad!
What matters if death be
Near? ah! be glad.
They did not see thy way,
Nor, didst thou seek theirs.
Let their voices sing thy lay;
Who knows? the eye that stares
At thee may be hers
Telling thee mutely, thou hast won at last!

Now, one more ring of laughter,
A moment's star-gazing,
Then let us hence depart, brother,

Wide ope' the doors of the future.
Ha! mad they name thee!
Bad not their hearts, it seems
Their life has its immortality,
While yours, an infinity of dreams.
Let flowers and faces fade;
New ones will blossom and the old will be dead

What dream-peacock, this moon,
With voice of silence,
Bejeweled with the golden stars,
With its spread fan, the tree—
What dance, this?
What rain-cloud hath it seen
In the sky of night's intangibility?

The sun sinks into an ocean of mist;
    The trees spread their green wings for flight;
A silence spreads over hill and valley;
    A pale moon leads the caravan of night.

The "star-traders" come from the desert of East
    With their loads of gold and silver;
As the breeze, that unseen camel walks along,
    Setting the golden western mists aquiver.

The last flicker of light fades away fast;
    Comes darkness, telling dewy beads;
The trees, shadow-like, melt into the sky;
    The drowsy West seeks to echo the silence of the East.

The Sunset-Images

The cloud-ships afire in the west;
Crimson, the surface of the lake;
The sun-brush paints the forest-canvas
In gold and green and red;
While the breeze-child turns the leaves of the trees
In the book of sunset-images for twilight dreams.

THE BELLS OF MOONLIGHT AND LEAF

The moonlight and the leaves,
　　Bells, these,
With tongues of silence;
　Chiming in silver, violet and green;
Ringing, rising, then falling on
　　The ground,
Set to weaving shadow-sounds
With the dark threads of sleep.

Like liquid gems pouring to a measure
　　Of perfume,
With shades of lavender tunes;
A dream-music of soundless sounds.

More than silence and sleep,
　　This bell melody
Of light, of air, and leaf,
Played by moon-bedimmed stars;

As corals in the deeps of a sea
　　Making
Pearl-harmonies with emerald tones,
To the cadence of an Eternal Dream.

Ah! more than Eternal Dream,
　　This moment,
A silver, silent tintinnabulation
Of the bells of moonlight and leaf.

　　　　　　　　　　　　　　　　DHAN GOPAL MUKERJI

Steps of rose
On rosier steps;
Thus, evening
Builds her staircase
Between sunset
And the infinite roof of space.

So our fancies
May fold their wings,
And walk on gleams
Of unending purple and pink,
Up to the blue pool. . .
And drink from its starry rim.

A Contrast

The sunset puts a necklace of cloud-pearls
Around the neck of the West;
Pink-blue veils, the gray mist weaves
For the East seeking sleep and rest.

Beyond the hills, the single star smiles like a blossoming flower,
As the moon silently pours her lullaby of silver
Into the ear of East, now fast asleep;
While the West's golden fever burns away its only star.

The star-hands play the harp of night;
Gold, blue, and silver the tones of its music;
Like soundless curves of dark and emerald-harmony
That golden-feathered swans of reverie make,
As they draw their trains of dreams across the pools of sleep.

The green hill, a priest with his hood of white mist;
The sky a conch-shell of turquoise
Through whose hollow the breeze calls the pilgrims
To this noonday worship.

Weary the soul of all things, this hour,
Save the bee, who, free from all thought of worship,
Visits her flower-lovers—
She too a devotee, in the honeyed sanctuary of Cythera.

Intoxicated

Wine of life? I have drunk of it!
Ocean of sorrow? I bathed in it!
Fountain of love! I have listened to it
Playing melodies
On the moon's many-stringed light.

The lake of friendship, I contain in my soul;
The river of joy has flowed into it;
And on the upland of my heart,
Dances dream-footed,
Song-drunk Radha.

Krishna, the player of flute,
The lover, the playful enchanter of hearts—
He has drunk of the wine of my life:
Is bound by the magic of my art.

Who am I? Maker of lute from the East,
Have breathed into it the soul that is God:
How can I do it? Foolish thy inquiry:
I do all!—I have drunk of the wine of life.

The rosy stream rolls down the hill;
Bareth her silver heart, the lake;
The tall trees, litter-bearers these,
Carry the goddess of dawn, who will lave her limbs
In the confluence of the lake and the stream.

"Festival of light!" chant the bird-priests.
The breeze chimes in ecstasy
Through the palm-tree on the lea;
The wicked sun steals a glance
At the Bacchanal of dawn from field to field.

"Arise, awake, see!" the barque of light,
Drifting through the hollow of the sky
In quest of the shadows fleeing far into the land of sleep;
While, stringing her lyre with sunbeams,
Nature plays her music of life.

The Flower-Girl

Rose or jasmine?
Champak or shephali?
Or a poppy-lamp with dewy flame. . .
What bringest to the Temple, maid?

Garlands of Shiuli,
That, dew-diamond-like,
The stars made on the green blades
In their own eternal image?

Is it a lotus,
The evening lily—
A star, that day leaves at night's altar?
Or the morning sun?

None of these?
Not the morning star?
Nor the white chalice of trance, the Dhutura?
What flower, then, for this dawn's altar?

A garland of thine emotions, these!
Ah! lotuses from thine
Endless lake of love;
And the sunflower of thy heart!

Music Within a Mirror

The lake, a silver mirror in a frame of green;
The swans on it but white fancies in a whiter dream.

The enchanted bowl of blue below the rim,
But a goblet with liquid diamonds, filled to the brim.

White within white, a song in a sea,
Painted within a mirror, green hill and tree.

Moveless music, without murmur or moan;
Swan-made curves, its tune, its measure, and tone.

Love's Inconsistencies

Why closed thou thine eyes—
    Two ever-lit homes of love?
Why heave sighs,
    Thou happiest dove?

Why dost sleep,
    When love awakes?
Why dost weep,
    When love merry-makes?

Why the sadness of Autumn
    With thy smile of Spring?
Why, with the light of morn,
    Night's darkening dream?

Oh, cease doubting!
    Open thine eye!
See, love knows no ending!
    Song doth not die!

Lave thy limbs in the stream of my song!
Why this cruel blessing, queen of my heart?
The source has ceased to be, many a day now;
The flow but a sand-stream, I know not how long.
O traveller after my soul, why call for the ferry?
Æons I waited to hear thy voice, to hearken to thee,
Thine arm chiselled and painted by God's own hand
To beckon me. Alas! the river of expectation
Is no more; the barque of joy doth not float.
Wilt lave thy feet? take my tears!
Come, goddess-guest, grant me this boon,
Before these eyes are dry—this soul a desert.

DHAN GOPAL MUKERJI

FLOWER OF DEATH

"Hast thou come? what hast
    Thou brought for me?"
      Asked she.
Then he, dreamt she, bent lower
    To bring the flower
    Nearer to her
Whitening, cooling lips and nose. . .
    Like fading rose
    Falling to repose.
"What hast thou brought for
    My bridal hour?"
    Asked a whisper:
Then his arms gathered the cold
    Body, death-cold,
    Whilom of gold.
"Sweet flower!" said she.
    Faded her last kiss
    On death's lips.

Eyes, sad eyes, what words they speak!
Words sweet as music—music that renders sadness sweet,
Have they all, the reveries, found their home in the eyes, thine eyes,
    sad eyes?

Rose

Rose has a life, they say;
Life that lives in day
Through night's darknesses.

Rose has a message to say
To you, to her, to they
That pray for her graces.

Rose has love to give away;
She gives it to the gay
And those that kiss her thorny tresses.

Rose is red, they say;
She blushes in dark and day
For lovers, unashamed, greet with kisses.

Rose has a heart, they say,
A heart that beats in May,
And when receiving Autumn's caresses.

Rose's soul, they say,
Is whiter than sun's day
That dispels life's dimnesses.

Rose is love's beauteous bay,
Lives ever, night or day;
Her smiles and blushes are our soul's mistresses.

The moon at the treetop;
    The green leaves a-tremble;
The golden glow's last throb
    With the call of the cymbal.

The Goddess of this hour,
    Peering silently through her star-woven veil
From her throne in night's aerial bower,
    While the chakoras* whistling, moonward sail.

What soft voices sing,
    Whispering strange messages of love!
What are those moon-eyes seeking?
    Is there no love above?

Love, let thine eyes speak to mine
    More silently than one star to another;
Pour thy soft smile like wine
    Into my mouth, thy lips on mine—thy lips so rare!

---

* Chakoras are the legendary birds of Bengal, who are supposed to fly to the moon and
suck honey from her heart.

On a Starry Night

The Milky Way,
That silver shadow,
Binds the heaven and earth
Like the chain of love.

The star-hosts, smiling guests of night,
Witness this meeting of love;
And my soul, in a silver stream
Like "the Way,"
Flows to meet them all
Across the ocean of night's silence,
Beyond the Universe's wall.*

---

* The Milky Way has different names in each language, it seems. The Irish call it "Leugh's Chain"; the Swedes most probably name it "The Silver Way"; the Hindus call it the "Shadow Path," and the Chinese call it the "Silver Stream."

The song-bird falls asleep;
The West, a silent song;
Timorous the breath of the breeze,
Like my soul at thy feet.

The eucalyptus, after bathing her hair in the pink-gold shower,
Puts a flower in it:
The evening star.

Shadows trip in from the East,
Like Bacchantes of nothing; as
Day breathes his soul into the night;
And my heart flows like a stream—

In search of a vasty sea,
Washing away life's impurity;
On it, drifts my love: a precious argosy!

A Picture

Emerald, the rim of the sea;
Purple sentinels, the hills;
The breeze half-dead or dying:
It is a song without singing.

The sun, the sweeper of the sky,
Washes it with the white of day;
For the moon, later, to paint
Her portrait of light and shade.

No sun-washed heaven that tells not of the moon;
No moon that doth not limn
Her frail, faery dream
On the sea's fluctuating rim.

One word the ships speak,
Only loud or low the tone;
One mist hovering about them:
A violet flute with lavender speech.

The waves sing a song, their own,
To answer the screech of the gull;
The sunset's fiery music
Breaks the heavens' blue lull.

Dance the golden cloud-ships
With sails of rose and silver;
While from the haven of the east,
The moon-ship weighs her anchor.

The sun-galleon has rowed downwards;
As our ships the self-same way;
The moon and her star fleet sail heavenward,
Following Night's trackless pathway.

Silver-footed dawn,
Treading the still air;
The sun-censer's golden fume
Tinting the turquoise dome,
Descends to the greenéd floor of this cathedral of nature.

The shy wood-goddess,
Vainly clinging to her vanishing raiment of mist,
With bowed head weeps tears of dew,
That overfill the flower-hearts,
Weeping joyfully, this hour.

Night's sorrow, day's joy;
Bird-votary's hymn of love;
The fading silence and morning star;
Man-child's awakening laughter. . .
What mirage, this, in the desert of my heart?

DANCE-WORSHIP

The breeze-spectator, still, awe-struck;
Falls not even the shadow of a leaf;
The trees, the meadows, the pools
Build the silent temple-hall for peace.
To the music of moon and stars
Played by the minute, and hour-hands of time;
Dances Nature's Night-Bayadere*
With the castanets of sleep and dream.

---

* Bayadere is the name given to a class of Hindu dancers.

Sun, moon and stars,
Chalices but these
In the hand of revelers,
That fill with fancies
Their crystal-white hearts.

In the blue's infinite tavern,
Have met our souls,
Each a luminous sun
On rainbow orbits dances and rolls,
Singing His Song, with His Love, drunk.

PLOUGHMAN'S SONG

Gold-dusty, saffron-robed maid,
What love brings thee
In the wake of the morning star?
Night's veil of silence
Thou tearest to fling away.

Laughing with such mirth—
The breeze thy playmate—
What playful mood, this? I ask.

What wonders dost thou see
From thine azure throne on high,
That I can not see from
My torn bed of straw?
I hear the roll of thy chariot wheels
On the red-paved pathway of the sky.

A man, I have not thy wing;
Old, worn, how can I fly from land to sea?
Beckon me not to follow thee;
Let me dream, let me lie,
Watch thy triumphal march,
And listen to thy soul-lifting hymn,
Sung by thy playmates that, lo! are winging the breeze.

Gone yesterday's rain;
Star-babies play in heaven;
The breeze that with clouds
Stole the moon, lies in chains
In the mountain's dark cavern.
The golden children of night
Raise their arms in joy,
As the moon-nurse opens
The nursery door of West,
And gives these the golden sun for toy.

The amber dusk veils the orange-tinted sea;
The coral-moon spreads silver wings
Like a gull, from a mysterious sea,
Follows in the wake of Night's star-laden argosy.

Coming of Dawn

Thin silver cloud-veils hide the moon,
The star-steeds of the chariot of night
Course for the western hills;
The west-wind a ceaseless flute playing,
With its stops of falling autumn leaves.

The forest and the valley a map
Drawn by the explorers in the land of reverie:
They color it with tones of violet and lavender;
Or, make rainbow waves of leaf and light
With tones from the changing palette of the breeze.

At last, the thin clouds become thinner yet;
The moon now a moonstone in an opal dream;
The leaves cease dropping, and dead the wind;
Begins a new measure, a new flute playing,
As the star-steeds' golden hoofs touch the western hills.

Thy world it is;
Thy music ringing;
Thy stars listening!
A wanderer, I.
Rest, oh, let me rest!
In peace let me lie!

Birth of Day

A cloud of agony thy face;
Poignant the silence of gray;
Lo! hear the golden cry that breaks it?
Rejoice! O Night:
Thy Child is born—
    The Day!

A Note About the Author

Dhan Gopal Mukerji (1890–1936) was an Indian American writer. Born near Calcutta, Mukerji was the son of a former lawyer who devoted himself to music and prayer. A member of the Brahmin caste, Mukerji spent a year living an ascetic lifestyle before enrolling at the University of Calcutta, where he joined a group of Bengali revolutionaries with his older brother Jadugopal. In 1910, Mukerji was sent to Japan to study industrial engineering, which he soon abandoned to emigrate to the United States. Settling in San Francisco, he joined the local bohemian community of anarchists and artists while studying at the University of California at Berkeley and later Stanford. In his time in California, he published two books of poems—*Sandhya, or Songs of Twilight* (1917) and *Rajani: Or, Songs of the Night* (1922)—and a musical play, *Laila Majnu* (1922). Mukerji graduated in 1914 with a degree in English, married artist Ethel Ray Dugan in 1918, and moved to New York City in the early 1920s. There, he embarked on a career as a popular children's book author, finding success with *Kari the Elephant* (1922) and *Gay Neck, The Story of a Pigeon* (1927), winning the 1928 Newbery Medal from the American Library Association for the latter. Recognized as the first popular writer of Indian origin in the United States, Mukerji struggled with marginalization and racism and regretted his exile from India late in life. Unable to return because of his youthful commitment to revolutionary politics, he supported the Indian independence movement with money and advocacy from abroad. Ultimately, he ended his life alone in his apartment in New York City.

A Note from the Publisher

Spanning many genres, from non-fiction essays to literature classics to children's books and lyric poetry, Mint Edition books showcase the master works of our time in a modern new package. The text is freshly typeset, is clean and easy to read, and features a new note about the author in each volume. Many books also include exclusive new introductory material. Every book boasts a striking new cover, which makes it as appropriate for collecting as it is for gift giving. Mint Edition books are only printed when a reader orders them, so natural resources are not wasted. We're proud that our books are never manufactured in excess and exist only in the exact quantity they need to be read and enjoyed.

bookfinity™

Discover more of your favorite classics with Bookfinity™.

- Track your reading with custom book lists.
- Get great book recommendations for your personalized Reader Type.
- Add reviews for your favorite books.
- AND MUCH MORE!

Visit **bookfinity.com** and take the fun Reader Type quiz to get started.

Enjoy our classic and modern companion pairings!

Classic & Modern